THE
INFINITE DREAM

THE
INFINITE DREAM

JOHN F. STEINBAUER

EDITED BY: CARRIE E. STEINBAUER

BALBOA.
PRESS
A DIVISION OF HAY HOUSE

Balboa Press books may be ordered through booksellers or by contacting:

Balboa Press
A Division of Hay House
1663 Liberty Drive
Bloomington, IN 47403
www.balboapress.com
1-(877) 407-4847

Because of the dynamic nature of the Internet, any web addresses or links contained in this book may have changed since publication and may no longer be valid. The views expressed in this work are solely those of the author and do not necessarily reflect the views of the publisher, and the publisher hereby disclaims any responsibility for them.

The author of this book does not dispense medical advice or prescribe the use of any technique as a form of treatment for physical, emotional, or medical problems without the advice of a physician, either directly or indirectly. The intent of the author is only to offer information of a general nature to help you in your quest for emotional and spiritual well-being. In the event you use any of the information in this book for yourself, which is your constitutional right, the author and the publisher assume no responsibility for your actions.

Any people depicted in stock imagery provided by Thinkstock are models, and such images are being used for illustrative purposes only.
Certain stock imagery © Thinkstock.

ISBN: 978-1-4525-3977-5 (e)
ISBN: 978-1-4525-3815-0 (sc)
ISBN: 978-1-4525-3816-7 (hc)

Library of Congress Control Number: 2011916957

Printed in the United States of America

Balboa Press rev. date: 10/17/2011

Acknowledgments

•　•　•　•　•

My wife Carrie, what can I say, words will never do justice. I look forward to the present and the glorious future. You are my light and hope, you lift my spirit and you were right: you are my soul mate and I'm yours! I thank you from my heart for not jumping ship and sailing for higher shores, you are a God send and an angel, thank you for forgiving me and loving me the way you do everyday. To my daughters, Chelsea and Kiersten, you are what inspired me to take this path and I thank you from the bottom of my heart. Without your true love and devotion I would have turned away and been just another story of heartache and a life that had so much potential. Your forgiveness and pure love opened my eyes to a new world of opportunities and your patience woke me to finally taking the path inward to my loving soul. To my parents, we have been through a lot, and you showed me that change can take place and growth can be accomplished with love, understanding, acceptance, forgiveness, and the possibility that we are all unique and we all make mistakes because that makes us who we are. Thank you for life and growing with me along the way. To my brother and sisters, we too have been through a lot and we have lost our way at times along life's path. I wanted you three to know I will always love you and I miss you very much. We all have our own path to take; I hope it is filled with promise, love, compassion, great health and the will to never give up. The door will always be open and I will always be there for you in the way you need. To my old friends and new ones today, we had a lot of good times and some that we wish never took place. I thank you for being a great listener, a shoulder to cry on, and a great friend when I needed you most. I hope I have done the same for you, even if some of us have gone our own ways. You are on my mind and in my heart always. I hope everything in your life today is remarkable and that love, happiness, patience, forgiveness and great health are blessed upon you and your loved ones. My transformation started with an educator who opened my heart to a book. It was through her personal struggles that I took the first step to be healed. I will never forget her. To the ones in my life that have passed on, you all have touched my life in more ways than you can imagine, I feel your presence from time to time and I know you are well loved in the place where only true love resides throughout eternity.

Contents

• • • • •

Introduction

● ● ● ● ●

This unique book that you are holding in your hands has no chapters. There are separators so that you can pause to take a moment to think about what has been written and how it applies to your life.

I constructed it this way for many reasons. One of the main reasons is that each one of you is different. We are all unique in the way we read, think, and respond to what we are reading.

You may read it straight through, stop at certain points to think constructively, or use this book as a guide when your life goes astray.

I hope that you enjoy the treasure you are holding and that your life becomes more profound, more rich, and more open and loving because of it.

We are all on this wonderful journey together we call life. Open your mind, open your heart, and take that first step!

This is not a self-help book in the sense that my way is the only way to approach life. There are too many of those books out there. The problem with those books is that they are written from the perspective of what worked for the author. While there may be great information written in them, it is possible that you will be led away from your true self.

We are all different. We think differently, we believe differently, we accept things differently, and we approach our own lives differently. This book is written for everyone who is lost, needing new direction, or is having a hard time with their own lives, from every religion, every culture, and every age demographic.

The world we live in is very difficult at times and can lead you away from your true self who is created from love. I believe that after reading this book you will become happier, more productive, more patient, and a better communicator.

We can all learn from one another. We can share our ideas, cultures, religions, spirituality, and who we are as an individual. We can also finally learn about ourselves from a perspective that heals us and leads us to a more loving, open, and caring life. We are the creators of our life; we have just simply lost our way. I truly believe in my heart that by reading this book, together you can find your way back home, finally stopping all the negativity that has enveloped you and blinded you from life's riches. It has been impossible for you to notice the miracle of life that has been generously given to you by choosing any negative path that inherently takes you from the loving self you truly are.

For those of you who believe in a higher power, guardian angels, masters, or any spiritual guidance, this next story is for you.

The Beginning of Discovery

• • • • •

One day about a year ago I was mediating and I was in a deep state asking for guidance with my book. For those of you who do not believe in a higher power, that is alright. We are all different. We think differently and we all believe differently. That is a great thing and not a bad thing as society will have you believe. During my meditation, this is what was said to me:

"Start seeing, not looking. When you do this, you simplify and finally start living. Life is so simple if you want it to be. How many times during your life have you searched for something you put down somewhere? You can not seem to find it no matter where you look and then finally you look and see that it was there in front of you all along!

Life's whole purpose is to overcome the obstacles that in turn make you a stronger soul. The problem is that we never take the time or effort to figure things out. The answers are right in front of us all the time, each breath we take. We decide to complicate our most simple task: ourselves and our lives. Life will always have obstacles. We are born with obstacles in front of us and die the same way.

You are already in a dream-like state, why haven't you chosen to make it come true? We all seem to get caught up in the fantasy; not knowing that you are in control and always have been of your own destiny.

Create your own solution, solve it and move on. Then your simple life will take over. When all the other distractions in life melt away you will find love in your heart, create it from your mind, and feel it from your soul.

We are the creators of our thoughts, as we are the creators of our emotions. If we simplify our lives, all thoughts will come from the heart where we find love, and it will feed your true self, your soul.

To simplify even more, you won't ever see life as an inconvenience. No matter what you are going through, it will be an opportunity, not an obstacle or a wall.

Only then will each day be perfect through your eyes, not the worlds. There will be no distractions, sadness, or confusion. Obstacles will be viewed as a good thing, not a bad thing.

Your life will finally become yours. What are you afraid of? All your fears fade with love. Are you afraid of being fulfilled completely? Think about it: is your life perfect now? Today is and always has been your day!"

The more I read this, the more amazed I am. I can not express this more sincerely and more profoundly to you. Life is overwhelming as it is. Why do we choose to complicate ourselves too? I was going to dissect each sentence, but I realized that I would be writing my own thoughts and ideas into it. I am going to leave that up to you. At the end of this book, I will supply you with poems, quotes and books that have helped me along the way. Some opened my views, thoughts, and ideas. Some made me take a look at myself more deeply. Others helped to change me along the way. I believe this book will do the same for you. We all need help at times. We all need someone to listen and to lend a shoulder to cry on. We all need a place to call home. But most of all, we need each other. Only in relationships can we grow, nurture, and heal ourselves from every aspect of our being.

Taking the First Step

• • • • •

To begin that journey we must start with ourselves. Do not be afraid; fear is from the mind. It is our ego that stands in our way from experiencing the all in life that is supposed to be enjoyed. You have to forgive the person for you to be able to move forward with life but you do not have to forgive the act or situation that took place. You can set yourself up to relive the act at a later date or time. Your mind will do this on its own by triggering that painful memory that can regress your progress. By forgiving the person, you can, with time, escape the pain that steals away the love and happiness your life would be experiencing. We seem to get caught up in the web that binds us into a dark world of depression, hate, frustration, sadness, and destructive pain.

In life there will always be outside influences that mold us into what and who we think we are, but it is ultimately our choices that make us who we are and will be in the future.

We are our own author, movie director, poet, and screen writer in our lives. Why not create a script that is full of love, life, possibilities, fulfilling experiences, and profound feelings of joy? The main reason we watch movies is to experience the character's life and to take us away from our own. Why create a script of hatred, sadness, strife, and ultimately depression or worse? The depression that robs us of any possibility of experiencing the all that life produces in front of us each and every moment of every day.

Life tests us all the time. The thoughts we create, the relationships we are involved in, the drama we dive into that can be the recipe for our own destruction. We all have great opportunities to rediscover our true self. We are all loving, beautiful people that transcend from our purest self, our soul.

Be Your Own Creator

* * * * *

Our minds and thoughts can be a dangerous place. Start today and notice the thoughts that pass through your mind and take the time to write them down. You will start to realize that your subconscious creates or invents stories in your mind that pull you into a mood of sadness even if you were in a perfect place of happiness or harmony before that time. Scarier yet, we often do this to ourselves intentionally due to the depressed mood we often create for ourselves. To explain further, we visualize a creation in our mind that traps us in the scene we have created in our minds. One example that took place in my life was thoughts of my wife cheating on me. Instead of me experiencing moments of love with her, the thoughts I created pushed me in a depressed mood for no apparent reason. Instead of me experiencing a blissful moment, I pushed our love away. Instead of us enjoying each other and communicating, I felt dread and my negative thoughts escalated with no merit due to the visions I chose to create from my mind. This is why people often argue and fight for no apparent reason. This leads to walls being created that often envelop us and keep us from the positive life we could be enjoying. More importantly, the beautiful relationships we could experience all the time.

Is changing our thought process easy? For some it will be easier than for others. We are all trying at our own pace to feel the love we have deep inside of us. For me it took a very long time of hurt, confusion, and a lot of sadness along the way. But I never gave up and I finally started to view life differently. I chose to want more out of myself and more out of my life. I wanted love to fulfill me and for my love to engulf the others who were closest to me. I basically learned to change by starting from the beginning. I learned to finally stand on my own two feet and take one step at a time. It took a lot of patience, a lot of tears, and most importantly being honest with myself. Think of it this way, if you continue to let life's drama get in your way or continue to live life in your head, there will never be an opportunity for even one true loving moment to exist. This is the wall or obstacle that is in your way. Move on, create another story line in your life, and start seeing your life the way it is meant to be lived.

Open the Door;
You May Be Surprised

● ● ● ● ●

For some people, including me, it is hard to communicate using words. However, there are many ways to communicate. For me, it is easier to write down my thoughts. From there, I can look over what I have written and think before I communicate my thoughts to the other person. Always remember to communicate in a constructive way, never out of anger, fear, regret, or by any other destructive measure.

There is a saying from a Snoop Dogg song that you do not have to be in jail to be doing time. Our minds do this to us everyday. We can put a stop to this by recreating our lives. We can only control ourselves, our thoughts, our ideas, our feelings, and the way that we perceive everyday life. To stop the negativity, stop making excuses! We all have a past, but it is what we do right now that matters because we truly do not know how our future will turn out. More importantly, if will get the chance to make the difference in the one's we love, including ourselves. Start living your life now, today, in this moment; don't ever give up on yourself, only you can make a difference in your life right now!

I have come to the conclusion that we are depressed, angry, destructive, and sick of life because we choose to stay stuck in our own negative quick sand. We get caught in our routine of life's dramas and move along as the years tick by, but stay the same by enabling our most basic needs. Relationships, love, and opening ourselves tell us that we are all different and we all are trying to find our way in this crazy maze called life. To sum it up, you are above your own creator… you! For those, including me, who believe God created us, look at it as God gave us life, but we are the creator of what we do with our lives. God gave us free will for a reason. He is letting you and I learn from our mistakes, love our own way, and create a life from our own beliefs. Simplify your life; that is the beginning of the new road. Then you will finally see, feel and experience what your life has been missing: a relationship that has new profound meaning and one that is complete.

Now, Start Seeing!

• • • • •

Be you. Flow with life and the beautiful moments it takes us all, then you are not against anything or anyone. You will not try to be someone you are not. You will finally be satisfied in the moment you are in, in your surroundings, and in familiar company. Where you are at all times will be neutral, not good or bad, you will experience the moment, be one with who you are with, what situation you are in and enjoy the moment in the present. Then your life's experience will come from love, your true self.

Freedom is a choice, not a certainty. Live your life like you are dreaming because only then will you look at everyone and everything as an equal. You will relax and enjoy where you are, what you are doing, and the experience you are having. Best of all, you will not worry about the mind's worst enemy, the why. When you are dreaming you are able to experience all of what you are feeling, seeing, and doing just as it should be in life. As I have and will continue to state, you are the creator of your own destiny. You are also the creator, writer, and director of your own movie. You choose the mood of the character you are portraying. While the scenery in your life may change constantly, the storyline will always be the same unless you decide to rewrite the script.

Stop thinking and start experiencing the all that has been given to us: life. We seem to feel that it is a bad thing when everyone has their own ideas, perceptions, passions, expressions, thoughts, and beliefs. What we keep forgetting is that we are all different yet we all have similarities as well. This comes down to freedom of choice and the fact that we all have our own choice to live the life we choose to live. However whatever life path we choose, we are all connected by life and the spirit we have in us all. We can only control our own choices; the drama in itself controls most of society's choices.

We all strive to fit in, but fit in to what? Ask yourself that question. By fighting and struggling to fit in, we all seem to lose our own identity; we seem to float on through our lives like someone floating through time and space. Not truly experiencing anything actually meaningful and profoundly real.

Being You is the Key

• • • • •

We seem to often change who we share our time with based on who is the most popular at the time. When this occurs, we become followers instead of equals. When we feel like we have to impress someone, we are often not ourselves in front of the person. We also tend to not experience the company for who they are and we do not allow them to experience who we truly are. We seem to just play the part but never truly experience the true sense of the moment.

It is great to experience all groups, cultures, religions, ideas, expressions, thought forms, and possibilities. Just remember, always stay true to yourself and let others have the opportunity to experience your true self as well.

With life, explore all possibilities and educate yourself daily without boundaries, then you can finally free your mind from the prison you have created for yourself. Why is it that we always want to change everyone else? We often desire to change cultures, to change loved ones, to change perfect strangers, and to change relationships? I believe that it is because we find it hard to change ourselves. We often feel that everyone else needs fixing, but the truth of the matter is that the only one we can change is ourselves. Be the judge of yourself if you may, but don't push it on others.

You have the choice to not assume anything. By making assumptions you get stuck in a rut of being for or against something. The trick is to proceed in your life with the assumption that you are living your own dream and you have the power and strength to stop any bad behavior you are currently taking part in. I currently have stopped several of my own bad behaviors by doing this. I have curbed alcoholism, racism, chronic nightmares and several other debilitating behaviors. You just have to want to stop these negative behaviors from continuing. By taking the first step, stop trying and stop the excuses. Simply put, put your words and thoughts into action. A major dark feeling will fade and a new light will envelop your whole body, giving you a more loving, patient, caring, and compassionate outlook on life. Remember, we all have a past. Some have been through worse times than others, but seriously, it is up to you and the choices you make that determine the direction of your life. We all have hurt ourselves or others in life. It is time to change the relationship. Forgive, be forgiven, communicate, and then move on.

Let it Fade

• • • • •

We imprison ourselves by thinking about our past. If you stop obsessing about the past and commit to a positive future, then you will start living a healthier, more nurturing and loving life now. Never give up! It takes time, patience and the will to make your life your own. The world will always move forward as life will continue to change, but it is your life. Create it and rewrite your own possibilities. One way that has helped me was being truthful to myself. Believing in me, listening to my heart, and loving from my soul, which came from the love of God, all helped to lead me on my right path. I was also given great advice and I chose to listen this time to my family, friends and the beautiful spirits that help guide me along the way. The relationships that help bond even the most lost souls. I spent a lot of time releasing all my anger and depression by taking time for myself, crying a lot, and understanding that we all have a past and we all come from love. I learned that the wall I had built was inhibiting me from experiencing the love that comes from within. I learned, as well as I am still learning and always will, to open myself to the greatest gift of all: life. I also learned to accept the choices that I have made, choices I am making now, and the mystery, magic, and belief I have now that I fear nothing. We are all immortal, we live on forever, and we are here to learn lessons that in time will bring us to a more beautiful place with God.

Remember, you are going to fail at life as much as you are going to succeed. It is great to view life this way because when you do fail, there is a new beginning, a new way to change your path and recreate your life story. It is important to recreate you and to learn valuable lessons that make yourself happier, more patient, and more compassionate.

It took a lot of thought before I could decide whether I should talk about my life in particular or to leave it out. After thinking it through for a long time, I have decided to briefly talk about a few aspects of my life. I really can not remember my childhood that much. I basically dug a hole and buried most of it. I did this for several reasons. I am not saying that my whole childhood was devastating and tragic, it was not. The person I became in my late teens, twenties, and thirties was a combination of my childhood tragedies and the darkness I let in to devastate me as well as all of the people I was close to. I was abused by several people in my past and then I became the abuser later in life. I am not going to state who the abuser was and it does not matter. As I have stated before and will state several more times, the past is over. Today is your day to move forward with your life; as well it is with mine. How I have moved forward is actually pretty simple. I just wish that I would have had the tools to move forward thirty years ago. I thank God everyday for helping me along the way as well as my guardian angels. The only way is to forgive not just the ones who abused you, but yourself for allowing yourself to be abused and then abusing others along the way. Believe it or not, we are all victims of some kind of abuse, whether it is physical, mental, sexual, emotional, and even at times, spiritual. Many people pray to God and do not feel as if they are heard. We then blame God for our own mishaps. God always answers our prayers in time. I am living proof that our lives are precious and are worth discovering and rediscovering. The true spectrum of life is often beyond our grasp of the way we think of it.

The main difference in my life from my past is quite astonishing. I had every symptom you can experience and I would let them constantly overpower me. Not just for a moment, a couple of hours, or a day or two, but for months and even years at a time. I was severely depressed, had major anxiety attacks, severe nightmares, extreme mood changes, was aggressive at times for no apparent reason, and had thoughts of suicide. Even with professional help I could not seem to unravel the web of destructive feelings I felt each and every day. Finally I realized that I needed help from a higher power. God does listen and so do his loving angels that help guide you along the way. You just have to be patient and be willing to listen from your heart and then you will be answered. For those of you that don't believe in God, you harness a higher power within yourself by slowing down and taking the time for you, this will be the first step you could take.

In my past I was blinded by hatred, anger, and destructive feelings. I thought that love was a joke and that being nice to anyone was a sign of weakness. The pathetic thing is that I was the one who was weak. Now even when I slip up at times

I fix the problem immediately, resolve it, and move forward. I apologize when I am wrong and I make things better. I opened myself to love and have never felt so much power and strength in my life. I have never felt so much passion, happiness, and compassion in my life. I feel open to discover all that life has to offer and I am thankful for the opportunity God has given me and you as well.

Believing

● ● ● ● ●

Always being you is the key! If you are forty years old and want to act like a goofball, then act like a goofball! If you are fifteen years old and have a serious personality, then feel free to be the serious person. If you have a shy personality, then be shy. No matter what, always remember that we are all different in the way that we think, how we believe, and what we want out of our own lives. However, we are all connected by the love we have come from and the love we share with each other.

I want you to think about this for a moment. It is a great thing that we are all different. Being different is what makes the world a great place to live in. Although we are all different, we are still all connected and everything we do matters. I can not emphasize this enough! Imagine a world without different ideas, different thoughts, different perspectives or even different choices. For some this reality is way too real.

I am astonished how different cultures believe as they do. How amazing it is to be a part of something so unique and heartfelt. I would love to learn and become familiar with all of the cultures of the world. I believe all cultures should be shared. We could learn so much from each other's beliefs. Look at it this way: what I am doing by writing this book is no different than what all cultures can do. Tell stories about how we pushed through our own walls, tackled adversity, and perceived experiences. Hopefully my story can help inspire you to write yours or help you through a very difficult situation.

Love is eternal and has no boundaries, it never sees color, race, or creed, it does not care what or how you believe, and it is not bound to anyone and comes from our actual true being: our spiritual self.

Stop Listening, Start Living

• • • • •

We all have that annoying voice that keeps us from moving forward. It is our ego that builds the walls and tells us to not accept love, peace, and happiness because these are signs of weakness. Our society in America is no different. We have a mentality that it is right to fight and not take any flack from anyone. We are also taught to step over people and to hurt others as they are weaker than us. How wrong can our ego be? How sad and lonely our lives turn out by listening to our minds. To be for or against anything is a true tragedy. The scariest place your ego can take you is within all the different moods it creates. I believe that a piece of heaven can be achieved here on Earth or you can create your own living Hell. It is amazing to me how we will take care of our lawns, our car, our house, our financial portfolio, and our careers, but we never seem to have enough time to take care of ourselves. We work so hard on our outside appearance and on material things that we seem to forget to work on the inside. If our inside is functioning well, then that will transfer to the outside, the physical you. I am not just talking about exercise, eating right, or going for yearly check-ups with your doctor, though these things are also extremely important for a healthy life. I am talking about living life passionately with love and caring about yourself and the others who love and surround you. It is also important to be empathetic and sympathetic toward others and to take responsibility for your actions and moods. By taking time for yourself and others, you will create peace and harmony in your life.

Change your ways, concentrate on your true self, and the rest is guaranteed to fall into place. Whatever you choose to concentrate on from your thoughts, your mind, or your ego, that is what will transpire in time. If you choose to think about lust, infidelity, pain, hatred, sadness, depression, and everything else that takes you away from yourself or the loving relationship you are in, then these things will transpire. The thoughts and fantasies in your mind will become the reality. The amazing and most spectacular thing is that you always have a choice where you want your life and your relationships to go.

Remember that being open to life is amazing. Do not hide behind the thoughts in your mind. They only prohibit you from loving openly and push you farther away from all that life can produce. The hardest part is the simplest part. We as humans keep trapping ourselves and pushing ourselves down the same painful path. Why is it so hard for us? Because it takes a lot of work and it takes a lot of patience to see ourselves for who we really are. We are the key holders to our happiness. We hold the winning lottery ticket and the most depressing part is that we do not even know it. Why is it that we will stop at nothing to own material things, keep up with the neighbors, and feed our lives with gossip, when all this does is blind us from the real feelings in life? We occupy ourselves as if we were blind, deaf, and uneducated.

We are blind because the truth is right in front of us all the time. The signs are right there: open your heart and you will finally see them.

We are deaf because our heart has been telling us about happiness, love, and eternal peace since we were born. That is the eternal voice which comes from your true self, your soul. It is the same voice that tells you how to achieve a happier you, but for most of us, it falls on deaf ears, a distorted mind, or even a crushed heart.

We are uneducated because we all have been conditioned to believe that if you do not see it, it must not be true. But you have something eternally that tells you differently. The sad part is that it has been with us all since we were born. We just seem to have lost it as we have grown. Just open yourself and let the love shine through. You can be a millionaire, have all the fame in the world, and purchase every new thing to your heart's content. But only love's meaningful relationships, lessons you learn, and open communication are the true things that will make you happy. I have known a millionaire that was severely depressed and hated his life. I have also known poor people that seem to have it all including love, happiness, meaningful relationships, and live caring, compassionate, and fulfilled lives. It does not matter where you come from or where you are now, make your life come from love and everything will mend together with the love you will openly share.

All Paths Lead Us Together

• • • • •

I do not practice a particular religion, but I am a spiritual person. Let me ask you this question. If God loves us all and we all come from God, then why are we so distant when it comes to accepting the ways others chose to live and believe? We should all embrace our beliefs as we should embrace all other religions, spiritual beliefs and cultures here on Earth. We are all God's children and we are created from his love. We are all different, yet we are on the same path moving at different speeds to our home. Some call it Nirvana, some call it the Promised Land, some call it Paradise, and others call it Heaven. Whatever you call it, we all end up together at the same place eventually. Why is it that we push our beliefs on someone when they did not ask to hear them?

I have touched the surface with various religions and have found that no matter what they are named they are all remarkable and beautiful teachings passed on through time. They all tell amazing stories, stunning adventures, and many of them tell us there is life after death. For some, they believe that we die with Mother Earth and our souls are set free.

Others tell us that we go through different dimensions to finally get to Heaven. Others believe that we are reincarnated until we learn not just our lessons, but every lesson there is to experience here on Earth. They are all amazing and they all could be true. I do believe in miracles. God gave us his miracle which is our life that we are living right now. I also believe in the concept of Karma. I believe that we all learn at different rates and the longer we take to learn these lessons, the harder our lives become by the choices we decide to make. I also believe that we take the mistakes as well as the accomplishments from our previous lives with us from life to life.

I believe that we are all connected and everything that we do makes a difference in our world as with the universe and to the other people we encounter along the way. Did you know that all religions at one time believed in some type of reincarnation? Look at it this way, no matter how you believe, why not share the beauty from your beliefs instead of hiding them away. Or even worse, cause hardship, war, or destruction. Can you actually tell me that God who created us all actually looks upon us and wants us to hate, be violent, and destroy what has been generously given to us all? Should we hurt others who do not believe what we do and live life through anger, hatred, violence, and wars? That does not sound like God; that sounds like man's way of destroying itself.

Please educate yourself about all of the religions on this glorious planet. Their beliefs may amaze you in the way that they are similar to your own beliefs. Some may not make sense at times while some will immediately click from the start of your reading. They all share one similar meaning and it is not fear, persecution, hatred, or destruction. All religions teach us about faith, to love and accept all, to learn from our mistakes, to help out those in need, to spread love and happiness, to cherish life and nature, and most importantly, to be a loving, caring, nurturing person to everyone without bias, judgment, or belief.

Again, we are all different; we all have our own ideas about life and how we should live it. Also, our beliefs differ about the afterlife and what happens when we get there. We also should understand that we think differently about every subject, idea, and thought process.

I strongly believe that we must start changing our ways now. The future can be positive and amazing but for some reason we keep pushing ourselves farther and farther from within ourselves. The simple answer is that it is up to us all. Everyone of us! We will all experience adversity in our lives or even a situation that will overtake us when we are not our true loving self. There is a simple way that may help you take the first step.

Create your own solution and then solve it. Finally and most importantly, move on. I will give you an example. Say you are an angry person who is sometimes abusive. You first must realize what you are doing, that you are the one doing it and that someone else is not making you act out in that way. Secondly, create your own solution to stop the angry, abusive cycle you are on. Third, solve it. This may take time or it may be solved quickly. Most importantly, move on and recreate yourself.

Being in the Moment

• • • • •

To be in the true inner moment is to be aware, but not concentrating on the moment you are in. Do not think at all, remember being for or against is the mind's worst enemy. Just feel, see, hear and experience all in that moment. This is a form of concentration, mediation, and a true heart felt moment. It is great to have time for yourself and to be deep in thought. Remember you are always in control of your thoughts and you can always move on to a more peaceful, loving, and caring time when in this process. You can also change the script of the scene you are viewing. You can change the outcome of that time as well. You are the movie director and the screen writer of your life. For example, when you are thinking that you should have been a better son or daughter to your parents, or a better father or mother to your kids, or a better husband or wife to your spouse, you can always change your thought process to your true self which comes from your heart and know that today you can be that better person. I always believe that it is good to look back but with restraint, knowing that you cannot change your past, you can only change the present.

Again, I cannot express this with a more profound meaning, simplify. It is the only way to move past the continuous struggles we put on ourselves. Live, love, and let go. When you let go of the past or hurt you have caused someone, then let the love in and feel, hear, and learn from your heart. You will finally be able to live your life in an honest, compassionate, and morally fulfilled way. Some people take longer than others and that is perfectly fine. But always remember that you are always in control of yourself, your thoughts, your memories, your feelings, and most importantly, how you want to perceive them.

It has been nearly thirty years for me to realize this. The worst part is that I hurt myself and the others around me during this time. The most prolific part is that I have finally made it! Now I am finally living, loving, and experiencing everything in life that is taking place around me. I have opened my heart, mind, and soul to another life. I thank God, friends, family, and myself for not giving up. Today and everyday that follows has been a dream come true. Not saying that everyday is without heartache would be not a true statement. I have finally realized that the struggle can be forever if you let it; you just have to tell yourself that you will not live in a depressed state any longer if and when it appears in your life. Say to yourself that today is my day and tomorrow is as well. Start living it and experiencing all that life brings into your heart. Start seeing the beauty that surrounds you wherever you go.

We as humans have the need to go backward and not move forward. Again, the mind does this for us if we want it to or not. The reality is that we can move forward by living in the now. In many relationships, the past seemed to be more pertinent than the present. Believe me when I say this, it is wonderful if your relationship is moving forward and you are truly happy, loving, and communicating well. Why conjure up something from the past that destroys all the progress the both of you have made together? Again, simplify yourself, the now, and everything that surrounds you. Remember that the mind's worst enemy is being for or against something. If you live through your heart you will then in return live from your true self which is your soul. Do not live your life one dimensionally. Open yourself to the three dimensional world that is in front of you. This is how to pull off the safety blanket we have carried with us for our lifetime. For example, try other music, foods, and hobbies. Try to open yourself to other experiences such as roller coasters, sky diving, and bungee jumping. Try new cuisines such as European, Eastern, and Indian.

Communication is the Key
to Open Any Door
That May Have Been Closed

● ● ● ● ●

There is so much to enjoy and to explore that will empower us back to our roots. Again, we are different here on Earth in the physical, yet the same eternally within ourselves, our souls that come from love. Why is it that when we strike up a conversation it is always with small talk? "How is the weather," "Hey, did you catch that game last night?" Why are we afraid of asking about the true feelings of the people that we enjoy this life together with? Why are we afraid to go deeper? Why are we so secretive with our deepest emotions? Why not speak from the heart when it comes to the true feelings we have, such as our dreams, beliefs, and goals in life? What scares us, what makes us happy, what depresses us, and what makes us angry? If we opened ourselves to better and more honest communication, wouldn't our relationships, love lives, and friendships be more profound, loving, and remarkable? Again, I am not talking about your deepest secrets; those are between you and yourself. If you choose to open that door, that is up to you.

We are afraid of being real and we are afraid of opening ourselves up in this way. Why? We are too wrapped up in the fantasy, the ego thinking portion of our minds that inhibits us to go deeper, to a profound feeling of living. Why can't you open yourself up to communicating about life, love, cultures, ideas, dreams, and feelings? Is it because you are too busy to listen? Or are you too afraid of hurting someone's feelings if you disagree with them? That is the magic of life. Remember that we are all different, we all think differently, believe differently, and feel differently. That is great and we should embrace this, do not be scared; communicate with an open mind, an open heart, and with a non-judgmental approach and the rest will take care of itself. You might be surprised that your relationship will bloom and reach a higher level. You might also find that we are different but we are all connected by the experiences we go through in life. You will also become a good listener. This may take time, especially for the male counterpart. It has been quite difficult for me at times, but I am becoming a more open listener and definitely a more openly constructive communicator. You will as well with time. Be patient and never stop believing in yourself. Today is your day!

With communication comes technology. While technology is great it is also damaging. The depressing part about technology is that we have drifted farther apart with the human loving connection. Yes, we can now communicate with someone on the other side of the planet but we have lost the connection that brings us face to face, the loving connection that bonds friendships and mends relationships.

Take a Moment

• • • • •

Visualize a world in which everyone opens themselves to share and love their own cultures, sharing their ideas and ideologies with their neighbors. Next, imagine a world that has no boundaries and opens their country to everyone. They share their beautiful heritage, cultures, and views. They also share their history, their lives, their passions, their feelings, and tear down the imaginary walls that close the remarkable connection we all share. Now, wouldn't that be an amazing world?

We may speak different languages, we may celebrate life differently, we may look differently, but that does not mean that we should keep up those negative walls that we think shelter and protect us. Learn to open up and share and you may surprise yourself by how small this world actually is.

We seem to feel at times that we have to defend ourselves. The way out of this is not to be for or against what is being said. What you can do is explain why you feel the way you do and keep an open mind. Listen and hear what is being said and enlighten each other about your own beliefs and move forward without judgment. This works with couples, parents, teachers, coworkers, friends, or strangers from across the globe. The bigger picture is the friendship and the love that comes from it. Words are just that, words. The connection between you and others are what counts. Open yourself and a new view of life will transform before your eyes.

Just imagine how much we can all learn and prosper as a world community from one another. We need to take the time to listen, hear, explore and finally tear down the barriers and enlighten each other with knowledge, love, and the desire to be unbiased when it comes to open communication. Communication is the key, it is all in the way we use it. There is the disastrous way by force and being destructive by our tone, or we can communicate by sharing knowledge in a constructive way that bonds relationships and brings us closer in a more caring, compassionate, and loving way. It is up to each of us; and the time to share, communicate, and be there for one another is now. The first step is to open the door to this idea and know that with time, all barriers small or large can be taken down. It takes love, understanding, compassion and a desire to heal ourselves and the hurt we have caused to one another. Communication is the key that opens the door and love takes care of the rest.

I strongly believe that we knowingly complicate and mask our feelings. We inherently hide behind our everyday lives so that we do not have to face our inner demons. We all have inner demons ranging from depression, anger, racism, and hatred. We are all born from love; we as humans create the hate. In a way, we have all been conditioned or brainwashed to believe these ways. What society does not tell you is that we are all different. Each individual person and each individual soul is different in some way. The worst part about not getting rid of your inner demons is that they seem to grow on their own, devastating you later with more force and pain. I personally lived through this as well as the unfortunate people who I lashed out on. You must want more from your life in order to destroy your inner demons. Just slow down, be more patient, and start seeing, feeling, and re-experiencing your life. By doing this, you will find your true self by opening your heart through love. You will finally be able to push past the confusion your mind feverishly creates.

In life you must face your fears. The easy way is through love; the hard way is to fight, become confused, and create the hate that evolves from this trap we put ourselves in. We all have our own ways to deal with the world, but ultimately we all overcome our obstacles through love.

Our history is ever-changing and is changing in front of our eyes as I am writing this. We discover, rediscover, and change our way of thinking by processing the new information we have found. We have written and rewritten history books and changed our minds time and time again about the topic of evolution and all the information we create by such discoveries. Why do we hold on to one belief in the first place when we know that everything constantly changes? Is it possible that we really do not know anything for certain? We only assume we do, or is the journey in discovering the true nature of our soul the learning, re-learning, discovering, and rediscovering the true essence of human nature?

Why do we label men one way and women another? We are the same, but most of us forget we have been conditioned to be different. Men are trained to be strong, emotionless, dominant, and brave. Women are trained to be passive, weak, emotional, and submissive. The Stone Age is over and it has been for a long time. If you think that we act the way we do because it always has been that way then we will continue to miss the big picture. Men need to be more nurturing, caring, and compassionate. Women need to stay the course and help out men who are struggling with their emotions. I know that men tend to be the aggressors but this is because of how we were raised. This does not mean that this is a good route to go or we as men should continue to fall back on always being the dominant one when it comes to relationships, business decisions, marriage, or other worldly issues. I am saying that men need to find their true selves through love rather than fall back on the excuse that this is how men are programmed. Together we need to communicate and tear down the barriers that have separated us from the beginning of time here on Earth. Women, on the other hand, should be more compassionate and understanding about the fact that in society most men have been pushed in a specific direction since childhood. This is not an excuse, but men need time to rediscover their more loving, open, compassionate, and emotional side. The time is now men, what are we waiting for? You can still be manly with the boys, but with your mother, sister, daughter, wife, or girlfriend, stop being the man and be the person who understands, listens, and opens himself to compassion. Men should have an open heart and be willing to give out the love that every woman deserves but seems to be missing. Have we made any progress since the first humans set foot on this Earth if men do not consider these important facts?

Men, start living life from within. Start opening your heart where the real strength comes from. Learn to be willing to give the love that is equal to a woman's but through time has been buried by all the pain, anger, and hurt we have caused since our history has begun. Again, not every man in history went down this path and some women in history were the aggressors too. Men can learn so much from the compassion, strength, and love of a woman. They can also model themselves after the gentleness, hope, and harmony from their hearts and the power, forgiveness, and empathy from their words, actions and emotions.

The true strength that a man possesses comes from their inner self. If men are as strong as they believe they are then why do they continue to treat the opposite sex like they do? Women want men to put down the armor, their insecurities, and their hate. We are the same, both men and women; men just need to catch up to women's more powerful inner strength. What is wrong with spending more time with your significant other or not watching the game so that you can be close to your wife, girlfriend, or daughter? Why are we not teaching our sons and daughters the ways of compassion, morals, and ethics? It is healthy to share feelings and to be open with people we are close to. Is there anything wrong with that? No, but for some reason men seem to be stuck in their ways because they have been taught to behave in this manner. This to me is a total misconception. I am just as tough now or even more so, but by opening myself up to my wife I have learned that I can be someone that sheds tears without hiding them and that I can openly admit I am wrong. I can be compassionate, trustworthy, and I can love openly without pushing others away. I can also help others instead of hindering them and I can express myself in a constructive way without hurting others. I can still play the role of protector and be the aggressor, but I do so in a more nurturing way.

As for women, there is not much to improve upon. Women have been patiently waiting for men to step up to the plate for thousands of years. The only thing I would like to say is to never stop being you. I am scared for women who choose a path that undermines the progress you have made. Also, if you choose to follow a man, then I am worried about your future. This is a difficult time for you; I see more and more females giving in to lust, violence, hardship and the pain that steals your loving, strong, nurturing ways. Men have dictated your every move for a very long time now. It is not a time to get even, but to open yourself even more and show men the way back to our loving hearts. This brings me back to my point. We are all different, yet we are all the same. We are all trying to find our way. Imagine if we just solved this. Imagine the love we would share instead of all the sadness we inherit now. We can learn so much from a woman's heart, the time is now for the opposite sex to open up to a new world of possibilities.

See Life Through Your Soul

● ● ● ● ●

Trust can be described as believing and opening yourself to someone or an experience. It is important to trust your partner, your friends, your children, and your parents. When you stop to think about it, you have to begin and end the cycle of trust with yourself. We have a tendency to put too much emphasis on the other people in our lives and forget to take a long look at ourselves. If you do not trust yourself, you will never trust anyone you come in contact with in this lifetime or any other. The basic principle is to open yourself to the expectation that trust is just a word and the real meaning is pushing through the barriers that you have accumulated. These barriers that we have make us feel the guilt, shame, and pain that push us farther away from ever trusting anyone. I used to say that trust is earned through time; that was so absurd. You should trust everyone you see in your daily life and every person you come in contact with, no matter what they are wearing, where they are from, what color their skin is, or how old they are. The only reason not to trust someone is if they are going to harm you. Think about a particular situation for a moment: let's say a person from another race robs you. Does this mean that everyone who is that particular race would rob you? No. You know that this is a ridiculous concept. But if we let our mental images be the controlling force in our life, it will hinder us from experiencing and seeing the truth that comes from our heart. We have been brainwashed too long to act in such a ridiculous way, yet this has been passed on from generation to generation.

We have decided not to trust certain people throughout history and we still do this today. We treat select people poorly such as African Americans, American Indians, people of low socioeconomic status, women, people with true psychic abilities, and an enormous list of people in different countries that I left out because the list would be insurmountable. We often do not trust other countries, different cultures, and their different ways and beliefs for no particular reason. Sometimes we choose to not trust our own government and our own neighbors.

If you learn to trust yourself, you will learn to trust others around you who deserve to be treated with respect. It amazes me that the world and its people are closer than ever before, yet we still separate everyone into categories by their different beliefs, skin color, religion, where they live, how they were raised, job status, education level, physique, sexual preference, fashion, and a mixed bag of titles we choose to put on the world. We even seem to micro-categorize everything in most societies, especially in the western hemisphere. Why? The simplest answer to most would be that we have always done so and it will never change. My solution would be that we should choose to move past this way of life and learn to take away the titles we put on everything and accept the people around us. To someone else you are different as well as they are different to you. If we move past this, the trust comes back to you and you learn to trust yourself. The simple way may be to choose to free ourselves from this way of thinking by believing in ourselves more and realizing that we may all be different on the outside but we are the same on the inside.

We are always changing. Every time a thought enters our mind, whether you know it or not, you change. We need to break free from what we look at, the judgment factor, and start seeing within ourselves. By doing this we eventually look beyond the person and see them for who they really are. This is where we are all the same; our true self comes from the spirit and the soul in each of us. No matter the color of our skin, where we live, our level of education, our social status, our sexual preference, our religious preference, our age, or our sex. This is the soul that lives on forever. We need to start realizing that we all have one goal: to open the door to all relationships, communication, to be non-judgmental and to experience the all in ourselves and everyone who is in our lives.

For example, if you see a large bald guy with tattoos running up to you in a parking lot, your first reaction would probably be to go back in your car and call for help or leave. However, what transpires is just the opposite. The man's daughter has fallen and needs help immediately. He was running up to you to ask if you could call 911. Another scenario: you see an old man sitting on a park bench each day you pass by on your way home. Your first reaction is to think how sad and lonely that man must be sitting alone there each day. What you have observed and why he is actually there are two different things altogether. This man is enjoying the outside, enjoying his time alone to clear his mind. Another example: you see a group of long haired teenagers skateboarding where you want to park your car in the distance. Your first reaction is to park somewhere else because those types of kids are always up to no good. You eventually park near the kids and the opposite occurs. The boys happen to be enjoying their activity and the friendship they are experiencing. You park your car and they smile and move on.

By looking deeper within yourself and trusting yourself you realize that everyone is different and that if we open our thought process to love, we in turn learn to trust everyone even more. Don't let the first thought be the one that you go with. Look deeper and the truth will come to you. There is something else you should understand: when we are born and first open our eyes here on Earth, we experience life at its richest, more purest and loving way. We all experience the true unbiased experience of true love. You experience your true self. You trust everyone without bias, you trust yourself, you love openly, you care about everything, you believe in everything your skin touches, your eyes see, your ears hear, even how your heart feels. You want to experience and know everything from a true compassionate way. You see everything through open eyes; you want to experience every culture, belief, person, nature, and what your new life has to offer.

It's Your Own Personal Choice

● ● ● ● ●

The only part that has a negative impact on this world has nothing to do with God, Jesus, or the Devil, only what man and women have done and what we continue doing. The state of the world looks bleak to most but not to me. We are always changing and the future is never written it is only changing through time from the ever changing ways of the human spirit. I think that we should have a day that everyone opens themselves to learning a new culture, a new way of living, and a new way of thinking. Then how about a week that we do the same, learn and open ourselves even more to the beautiful possibilities out there. Then we could even do this for a month. We could take turns going to different countries, learning a new language, making new friends, trying new cuisines, and even extending our families. Then why couldn't we do this for a longer time, how about a half year, three quarters of a year, why not a whole year? Imagine how amazing it would be to open the man made walls we have chosen to build so high. To learn, experience, and enjoy a new culture, to actually touch, smell, and see places you only experience on television or read about in books. Imagine how humbling it would be to know we all suffer at times, we all feel pain, we all cry, we all get depressed, we all want more out of life. How astonishing it would be to learn that every culture is unique, intriguing, beautiful, full of passion, and remarkable in its own way. Imagine how we could all help each other, not just in a crisis or time of need, but everyday. We have become closer through technology but we seem to completely walk backward when it comes to opening our hearts to experiencing what we all have to offer. Since the world is struggling with the economy, wouldn't this be a great step to help move us forward?

I was going to write about society as a whole, but I truly cannot do this for the simple fact that I do not know how everyone lives their own life. I do believe that everyone is entitled to freedom of choice and the freedom to express themselves. And I know that with the world out of control at times, governments believe they are protecting people by pushing more laws, rules, and other means of expressing themselves. I do know for a fact that if we learn to overcome these fears we have chosen to overwhelm us, then and only then will we finally see everyone for who they truly are: the same as you and me, but different in the way we choose to live.

You can control your mind; do not let your mind control you. Seize the moment and do not let your mind run rampant. It is easier said than done, but with continued change of thought, your mind can be free of the daily conduit of thoughts that each day pulls you in directions farther away from your true self. We are all strong, loving, caring, compassionate, and thoughtful souls. How can this be done?

Each thought, especially the negative ones, that enters your awareness should be viewed and then a decision should be made whether it is worth keeping or not. It is the awareness first, then looking at the thought from a higher perspective or from outside the box. Decide if the thought is worth going over or if it is better to let it pass. The mind subconsciously filters thought unknowingly into your view. It is being aware of these rampant thoughts and deciding where to place them that is important. The bottom line is if it makes you feel sick, sad, destructive, or frustrated, I would advise you to let the thought pass or face the problem, solve it and then move on. We get caught up in the drama of life so many times that we let it play in our minds. If we could separate the drama for just a day or a week, we would be amazed by how much time, effort, and hardship we have caused to ourselves as well as the relationships we are in. Let it go, let yourself and your relationships thrive from the heart, live from the feeling and let the mind be set free so that your life can feel and experience the rest. To get started take some time out of your busy day. Sit in a room alone and shut your eyes and the mind will do the rest. Then it will be up to you to personally attend to those thoughts as you may on your time.

One example is when my wife and I were invited to a party. I used to not enjoy meeting a bunch of new people, but I said yes anyways. That whole day was a disaster for me and whoever was near me. I remember letting my mind conjure up all of these ridiculous scenarios that I thought would happen. That day I became agitated, depressed, and pushy. This is when I didn't know how to stop this bombardment of feelings and thoughts from happening. I kept thinking about how I wouldn't know anyone. My wife knew these people and I would be left alone. I also thought about how long the drive was and other stupid things. To my amazement, I had a great time! I had a lot of fun, the food was great, there was a lot of stimulating conversation, and I made several new friends. When I look back at this time, I am so glad how I have now learned how to let go of the negative thoughts in my head and sustain, nurture, and build on the positive ones.

Being Complete

• • • • •

I have heard people ask, "How do you know when you feel complete, and you feel all that life offers us each day?" I usually tell them to remember when they first told someone they loved them and they responded back to them with the same answer along with enthusiasm, love, and tenderness. Some people call it being on cloud nine, reaching that higher level that consumes you with a feeling that can never be expressed in words. When you reach your true inner self, where the soul is attached, you find your true loving spirit of nature. When you feel complete it is like when you first kissed the love of your life, when at that time the world seemed to melt away, that all your troubles vanished and all your senses were blended into one. When time stood still and you were in complete bliss. Even if the world around you was in complete chaos, nearing the end, you would be happy and complete while experiencing this. This is the closest thing I could use to describe that feeling: when time stands still and you are in complete awareness to the love you feel around you. Everything you see, feel, smell, and touch is different.

Everything is experienced from love; the only true feeling that I hope everyone has the chance, choice, and passion to discover. I wish I could tell you more, but this action comes from just that.

Tear Down the Walls

• • • • •

We all have trouble communicating and listening at times during life. The main focus or objective of communication is listening with full attention to the words being spoken by the communicator. It is also important to not fall into the trap of being for or against of what is being said by the communicator. Learn from the words that are being spoken by the communicator and then let it be. Do not express the feeling of being for or against that your mind is programmed to do; just listen and then move past it. Unless the communicator asks for advice or what you think about the topic being spoken about, move past it. Even if they do ask for advice, be non-judgmental and do not be for or against the topic. We seem to get stuck in the rut of trying to change everyone. We seem to believe we are the one who is right instead of listening and communicating without judgment. You must get past this and realize the truth from the maze of confusion. Remember that everyone is different. We all have lived different lives, lived different experiences, have different thoughts, and we all have been searching at different times for the answers that only we as an individual can seek and find. We need to remember our simple self; the one that opens him or herself to everyone, to every experience, the laughter, the joy, the happiness from within, the love that only comes from our true selves. Do I have the answer for you my friends? I wish I did. As we are all individuals, we all need to find these answers from ourselves as individuals. How bad do you want to be freed from the depression that clouds your vision, darkens your mind, swallows your heart, and pushes your soul farther from the truth?

The truth will set you free, but only if you are truthful to yourself. One by one each demon, each hurtful act, and each regrettable decision that haunts you on a daily basis will finally fade away. If there was research conducted on everyone who ever committed a crime or who was incarcerated, you would find that each person was abused in some way before they committed their crime. The problem with our society is that we never stop the abuse and never take the time to try to end the cycle. We are so caught up with our own drama that we never ask the simple question, "Can I help?" Remember, it is ultimately up to us to want help, but try to imagine a society that reached out and helped, loved, cared for and accepted people for who they are. Again, we all have done things in our life that we regret, but by changing the present time we are now in, we hold the key to reversing the pain we chose to push on the world.

Take the time to look deeper and see the true person from the view of the soul. What we tend to forget is that we are not perfect, we never have been, and we never will be as a human being. We are here to learn, to open ourselves to the only true thing that matters which is love. As soon as we are born into this world we are thrown to the wolves. We learn from a young age that violence is normal, pain is something you will always have to live with, and hurt will always be a part of your life. The sad part is that it does not have to be this way. We just need to take a few basic steps to open the door to communication, open ourselves to want to love and to want to be there for the person next to us. The only way to set yourself totally free is to open the door to your heart. There is nothing more painful to see than all of these souls in pain when they do not need to be.

What deeply saddens me is that we do not take the time to realize that most of us are digging ourselves into an early grave. This subject has been studied, analyzed, and dissected over and over. Stress, anger, sadness, revenge, depression, and anxiety all lead to an early grave. Most of us do not realize that we as individuals have the power, strength, and ability to create a new life from the love we harness from our true unique self, our soul.

I also mentioned previously that I believe in reincarnation, or simply put, that we will incarnate at different times in the physical world to learn valuable lessons that will bring us closer to our true selves and to our home with God.

I believe that if we do not learn and put forth the effort to make a difference now, the next life we have will be filled with more grief, sadness, and difficulty. Look at life here on Earth as a pyramid. There are a lot of us that are on the bottom trying to find ourselves and are falling short of our expectations. We seem to get stuck in the same ruts, believing we are all alone, only to push us farther from our true path of happiness. This is a place where most people are. There is no communication and everyone is out for themselves and

Looking Outside,
Seeing From Within

• • • • •

I am sickened that we choose to deceive and purposely hurt ourselves, families, friends, and loved ones to supposedly get ahead. Why do you think that we are so far apart now, so alone, so untrusting, and so sheltered? Because we seem to think that the others in our life are only hindering our progress. If progress is defined as hurting, stealing, lying, cheating, and destroying, how can you look me in the eye and honestly say that this is a positive thing? True progress is made from trust and from learning lessons through relationships with others, not just in the safety of our friends and families. Let love be your guide. Let the true feeling that lifts you from wherever you might be in your life help lead the way. If I can do this, there isn't anyone out there that cannot truly achieve complete peace in their own lives. We came to this planet with it but we seem to have lost it along the way. The realization is that it has been with you all the time. Ask and you shall receive. Open your heart and there will not ever be a door closed. Let your soul take over and life will start to make sense.

For the first time in over forty years, I have arrived to the realization that I have finally seen the light. I still have much to learn as we all do, but everything has become so much easier for me along the new path of my life. The great thing is to notice what is going on in your life and to readjust your ways: how you think, what bothers you and how to fix it. Open yourself to everything, weed out the areas of your life that drag you down, and become your own guru. We all have the answers, just slow down, listen for the answers and you will be surprised how everything will become that much simpler.

Do not get wrapped up in the toxic perceptions others push on you or the ugly perceptions we have of ourselves. Each day is a new day; a new day to discover what you have been missing in your own life. I know from experience that the longer you travel down that scary path of resistance, the harder it is to clearly see the love we all have. I am telling you that today is your day to try, not give up, and restart your life. I do not care if you are five, fifteen, thirty, fifty, eighty, or even a hundred. If your life is full of hate, depression, sadness, and pain, you have the power, strength, and love to change. Change today and make tomorrow's chapter a new one full of the possibilities that lift you to a new path of pure joy.

Remember that each one of our lives is like a dream, a movie, a script, and a book. Life is drama here on the physical plane where we as humans feel everything from the five senses we were born with. The problem is that when we live within the fantasy we lose the ability to cherish these senses and no longer use them to benefit our lives. We seem to lose that need and what we experienced as a child.

We could learn so much from children if we would just take the time to listen. When you are a child you live life through experiences and open yourself up to feel everything that could be learned from the experiences themselves. Confusing as it may sound, children love unconditionally. As an adult and as we grow through our teens, we lose that special magic that we were born with. We lose the openness to believe in ourselves, to believe in others, to love everyone, and to never judge others. We seem to let these fulfilling attributes escape us as we grow and let our minds fill with a mass brainwashing of someone else's ideals and beliefs.

Children learn from a higher perspective. They believe in everything and seem to know that anything is possible if you just choose to believe in it. We as adults push our beliefs, our pain and our hardships on children. Then as children grow, they learn all the bad habits of our world and start the trend once again. It is a vicious cycle. You think we would learn to just listen and learn to take the time to sit and see how our lives look from a child's perspective.

I remember adults telling me when I was a younger that I don't know what love is, that you have to be older to know what it truly is. What a bunch of malarkey! At a young age, that was true love at its greatest! That was the purest love, until now, that I have ever felt. That puppy love feeling that all my five senses experienced, that crazy, all inspiring feeling that never seemed to stop was true love. I am so lucky to have this feeling today at forty years old that most people never have again. That first love was magical; everyday was new, exciting, and full of adventure. It seemed as if time stopped and only the two of us mattered in the world. When we become adults, we seem to disregard those true feelings and we live from the fantasy in our heads instead of the love we could experience from our hearts. This is when relationships become tiresome and tend to lack that magic they once had.

Remember when the simple touch, the simple look, and the simple pleasure of the heart lured two people in love closer than any dream or fantasy you could imagine? This is where simplifying comes in once again. As an adult we tend to constantly worry, which creates heartache and problems from the thoughts in our mind. Start experiencing each other from sight at first, second experience touch, and third experience the feeling of the connection between you two. After that, push all barriers away and enjoy each other from your heart that is full of love which connected you two together in the first place.

We should learn from the younger souls that are in our lives. They live in the pure, loving, and fulfilling way that we are all supposed to live. We seem to brush the young off; instead, we should learn to listen and experience life from their viewpoint. We could all learn so many valuable lessons and finally break the cycle of madness that we as adults seem to so easily push on each other.

Just a Thought

• • • • •

Many people believe that God is angry with us and feel that the end is near. They feel that God is devastated by our destructive behavior, our anger, and our sins. I actually believe the total opposite. I feel that God is saddened by our behavior as any parent would be if their child decided to act inappropriately, if their child hurt them purposely, or if their child went down the wrong path and eventually hurt themselves. I believe that we ultimately have chosen to hurt ourselves. We have selfishly, destructively, and purposely journeyed down the wrong path while crushing, stepping over and through anyone to achieve power through greed. It is our own doing from the smallest act of destruction to the largest one. History will never change unless we choose to change it. The world must unite as one to push past these barriers that have caused so much hurt, pain, and sadness. For those who believe in a higher power such as God, if he can forgive us, why is it so hard for us to do the same? I bet you cannot come up with an answer, especially an answer that is from love, truth, and conviction.

Why can we not truly appreciate life? Why do we always seem to seek out hardship and live through those means? Why can we not open ourselves to a new way of thinking, living and loving? We need to build upon the rubble and lay new ground, a fertile soil of hope, gratitude, and openness. A world that shares, lives, laughs, cares, and learns from one another all of the possibilities that our beautiful planet has to offer. Whether you choose to believe in God or not, it is your responsibility to push past these barriers and live together as one big family. We either destroy or create; we either listen or turn away.

The Story That is Being Told
is Exclusively Yours

• • • • •

What makes me upset is when people get angry when others tell lies. Let me clarify that I am not talking about situations such as someone cheating on their loved one and getting caught and lying about it. I am talking about the stories being told and the perception we conjure up from what is being said. Think about this: we actually, in one form or another, exaggerate all the time, every day, in each story we tell. If you want to call them white lies, fibbing, or exaggerating, it is all the same. Each person will perceive the situation differently. Try this exercise: tell a story about a picture taken of you a year ago. Every time you tell the story, it will be told in a slightly different way. You are technically lying each time you change your story. Try this: during your day on a weekend or at work, let a couple of hours pass, then try going back and explain your day to someone. Tell them what you did, where you were, who was listening, what was said, and what emotions you were experiencing. Explain these feelings to several people. If you told the story three times, it was most

believe so, because if we can so easily spread disaster, hatred, racism, fear, and separation since mankind inhabited Mother Earth, then I believe we can also learn to choose to open our hearts and minds. We must instead choose love, kindness, empathy, compassion, and forgiveness. Only then can we learn to be the souls that view everyone and everything as equals.

Instead of looking at a country, simplify it into a beautiful region. Instead of looking at a region, simplify it into a spectacular culture. Instead of looking at it as a culture, simplify and look at them as precious human beings. Instead of looking at them as precious human beings, simplify it and look at them as people like you and me with a heart, mind, and soul. Instead of looking at them as just people, look at it as these people have families and friends. They laugh, cry, and hurt as we do. These people have stories that may be spoken in a language that we do not understand, but it is still spoken from a person with a heart, mind, and soul. Reach deep into your heart and your soul will finally push away the years of insecurities and open your darkened, deceived, and conflicted mind to an utmost certainty of pureness; the pureness we all have instilled into us from the time we were born. It does not matter where you live, where you are from, what you believe or do not believe or what you want from your own life. We all need each other and we all have something to offer each other. We just need to want to change. Remember that there are no quick fixes. It takes dedication, hard work, and the will to change. We have created this mess; it will take time to clean it up.

It all comes down to basics. How hard do you want to work at being unified and complete as a person? We all have, at times, lost our way. As a society and as a world we seem to do this without any consciousness of what we are doing or of the consequences along the way. For you as an individual, this is where it all begins. We have taken the gift of life and made it into a burden. We have made a dream into a nightmare. We have made the one all inspiring gift of communication into words with no meaning. We have made a world with so much color and beauty into a world of dullness of grey and dread. We have commercialized and labeled life and boxed and sealed how we should live our own life. How can we tell another how they should believe, think, and feel? I cannot even contemplate this way of thinking. Again, we are all different in the way we feel, think, and believe.

Since humans have communicated, we have endured differences with each other. Back in the day, communities would separate themselves by their beliefs. Now we live closer to one another and live in societies that have many beliefs, ideas, and feelings. But instead of making this a precious miracle of positives, we have made it a nightmare of disasters, one after another. This is the miracle that has slowly faded through time. No matter what your beliefs, we should live as equals. For those who believe in God, he created us all as one, to learn and prosper from one another, to open ourselves to the love we all share. We should be enjoying our differences, learning new exciting and amazing things, exploring new astonishing places, loving the cultures that you inherit, and learning to love beyond what your mind holds you into thinking. We seem to pull ourselves away from what we have been born with; a life of choice, a life of love, and a life that can lead you to whatever you want it to be.

Love Has No Boundaries as Well as Fear

● ● ● ● ●

Fear with many overwhelms their being, especially in relationships. We, as in life, build this imaginary wall that not just blocks out anyone from ever getting in, it glorifies the ego in falsifying and protecting us from ever getting hurt. First of all, all lives feel pain and sadness, and broken hearts are just a part of it. We are here to learn lessons as well as feel pain. But with sacrifice and the time you have spent here on Earth, why not try to make every moment with your significant other worth living for? Live every relationship you are in with all five senses. You should experience life and the people in it as if they will not be in your life tomorrow. Fear and ego are a part of everyone, but you do have the choice to ignore them and let them fade from your being. If you live your life from the perspective of love then your life will be just that: lived from, opened up to, filled with, and wrapped in love.

Most relationships I have seen and experienced tend to be lived externally instead of internally. By using all five senses, you experience the relationship through your heart. You open yourself up to the moment and join the process that governs the initial time spent. If you are in tune to the all in that moment, then all fear and negative thoughts tend to take a back seat to your true internal feelings.

You must stop looking at love as something weak, something you do not have time for, or something that will only waste your time or eventually bring you down. During our life span, we let ourselves down as well as we pull ourselves up. Love has nothing to do with it. Either you want to be fulfilled or you choose not to be. Fear is the wall that traps you into a world turned off from the rest of your existence.

By using the five senses, the tantric, endless, and heavenly moments will occur more naturally. With this unlimited and boundless way of pure enjoyment, it does not matter if it is your first date or your 50th anniversary. You will experience more passion, joy, openness, communication, and love than ever before. You will experience each other by sight at first. This is what attracted you to each other in the first place. The moment you looked into each other's eyes that feeling of completeness took over. Use this feeling every time you are together. If you see from your heart, then you will always view that person for who they are. Let the rest of the world fade and seize the moment from within. The second way you will experience each other is by smell, another attractant that turned your heart inside out when you first met. The third experience is, to me, one of the most important: touch. This is probably the biggest reason you two got together in the first place. From the simple touch of your hands to the time-stopping kiss that brought you to your knees. I feel that most relationships die because of the lack of touch. Remember when I mentioned that we seem to live life in a fantasy? In this regard, bring the fantasy out in your relationship to spice things up a little. Touch is felt from every aspect of our being. Due to the fact that we are living in a physical world, touch should be more emphasized in relationships. One thing that has greatly improved the closeness in my marriage has been to give my wife daily massages. We kiss more than we did when we first met, we take bubble baths together, we hold hands more and hold each other every chance that we get. This has also helped to open doors to our communication as well.

The fourth experience is communication which happens to be the key to seriously understanding where the other person is coming from. Remember that we all think differently, have different assumptions, hear differently, and have different feelings. By opening yourself past your ego and fears, your position on communication will evolve from a higher perspective. You will appreciate and enjoy communication from a constructive form that builds the bond and nurtures the relationship as a whole.

The fifth experience blends in with the fourth, from communicating to actually listening and hearing what is being said. I will admit that this was the hardest for me to do. Looking back, there was no way to say this other than I really never tried. By hearing every word and listening to the story that was being told, truly listening opens up a new world of possibilities between you both. Hearing is the essential piece of the puzzle and doing this ensures that love is being felt and absorbed from your energy. When your energy is fulfilled your partner's will be as well.

The sixth experience is one that only arrives when the moment is complete between you both. The sixth is a feeling like no other, an unexplained moment when all your surroundings vanish into thin air. This is when true love is reached and your soul is finally awakened. In that moment, your partner's soul is awakened as well. At that time nothing else matters but the moment you are in. Just remember that by being here on Earth, the sixth experience is reached but not acquired to be with us always. It takes dedication, love, understanding, peace, trust, patience, and an ability to move past any indifference. Remember that you are still going to have bad days and days that bring you down. Even with these days upon you love will open all doors that lead to your heart, the love from your soul that is within us all.

The miracle is the beauty of experience, the beauty that is present everyday, and the beauty that we all share within ourselves. We learn from a very young age about the sadness this planet has succumbed to from the continued hardship of conflict, war, and destruction, yet we continue to push away love and harbor hate. We continue from generation to generation to teach about pain, struggles, and anger instead of ending this cycle of frustration and teaching something new, fresh, and open minded. Fear has no boundaries; it consumes individuals, communities, cities, countries and the individual beliefs in your heart. We could teach something that pulls people together from all walks of life, from all cultures, perspectives, and ideas. I like to think outside of the box. I love it here because I live my life opened to the idea that my personal way is unique and the world is my window to the gift we all share. This has also helped me push fear away, open all doors, break down all barriers, and open love from within.

Push away your ego and reach in through your heart as it was when everything in your life is clear. That every new experience was better than the last. This is where the secret is held; the key to everything pure, good, and healthy. Your heart is the child inside of you, where everything comes from love. The only pure atom is your body. Where all reason, feeling, inspiration, and belonging comes from. With practice, by reaching this state through meditating, regressing, or just in deep concentration, you will be lucky enough to share this moment of heavenly energy. I believe that we are here to experience everything. However, this does not mean we have to experience hate, wars, deprivation, and other negative emotions.

The amazing ability we all have in this world is the choice to change our ways at any time. Some will take longer, some will fall as much as they get up on their two feet, and others will not listen to reason or try because they assume that this is the way it is supposed to be. None the less, we all have the choice everyday to make a difference of who we are, how we will act, and how we will leave our footprint on the Earth. You already have the gift of life, why not use all your resources to make your life stand out and be yours from the love you already have instilled in you? Believe me, when you experience this heavenly place, you will be overcome with the ability to want to change.

Opening Your Mind

· · · · ·

Remember that there is a difference between thinking about something and worrying about it. It is the same for believing in something and reacting to it. When you think about something, the thought enters your mind and then the natural reaction is for the body and mind to respond to it. For example: you have a major test in a week so you prepare for it by taking notes and studying. That is the thinking side; the normal reaction is to worry. You think thoughts such as: did I study properly, did I miss some notes? You need to differentiate between the thought entering your mind, the thinking part, and the negative thought that is taking over, the worrying side. When you worry, you push aside all you have learned, all the time working diligently on the task at hand and you will falter and waste time on the thought. Do not be for or against, let the thought enter your mind and then move forward and release it.

Release the burden of dwelling on anything, especially negative things that lie in your head. Just make a decision about it and move forward. Answer your mind's question:

yes I will, or no I will not. If it is something that you cannot answer, then let it go. If it comes up again then make your decision. By doing this, you will have more time for yourself and more time to see the beauty that surrounds you. This is the same lesson with life. Believe it or not, you make most of your decisions without even knowing it. For the decisions that linger and take you away from your life you need to respond with a yes or no and then move on. Remember that your life is yours to create. As I have stated before, you are the director, the writer, the actor, and the creator of everything you do, say, believe, and portray in your life. It is always you. There are outside forces that may take you astray, but it all comes down to the choices you have made and what you do with them.

Your Pureness is a Unique Experience Shared With the Entire Universe and Every Soul's Light

● ● ● ● ●

What we mostly forget in our crazy and adventurous lives is that we think there is some perfect way that we should live. We strive to be on top, to win, and to overcome pureness that we mistake for perfection. With pureness we are already complete. We live our lives from the passion we experience from within. Perfection is the way of awkwardness, it is the feeling of never being fulfilled and complete. It is living life from another's perspective, their agenda, not yours. When we do not live life from within, we shun the world, become rigid, unkind, and look at life as a never-changing heartache of confusion.

How many times do you go though a day with the attitude of just wanting to get through it? For example: playing out the day in your mind, looking forward to a certain time, that certain moment, a vacation that is months away, the weekend that is arriving, or waiting for the moment when your life will be better? Just imagine how many minutes, hours, days, weeks, months, and years have just passed by and been wasted. How many lessons could you have learned during those times? How many beautiful moments are now long gone and faded, how many experiences are lost, never to be regained?

Your life is yours to live. If you do not like something you are doing, a career or job you have, or a relationship you are in, only you have the power to change it. Make it better, try harder, try a different approach, or if there are no other options, just move on. You make the decision. This is your life today, tomorrow, and in the future. Surround yourself with people, places, and things that make you happy. Why live in misery or live one waking second in a mode of life to just get by? Society does this enough in our lives by giving us boundaries. Why would you ever put boundaries on yourself and pull yourself further away from love, compassion, happiness, and the desire to live your life completely? Every fiber of our existence is purified from the love we all share and have instilled deep within us that we share with the universe.

Remember this: you as a human, on this physical plane, can never be perfect. But your life can be! As a human we always make mistakes, but as for our lives, we can always make changes and we always have the choice to learn from our mistakes. That, in turn, makes our lives perfect.

Why Not?

• • • • •

This is the time that I want to get a little negative. I cannot seem to fathom the idea that we as a species are supposedly more advanced than animals. Adults in the twenty-first century cannot seem to teach our children to help anyone who is in need. We also ignore the fact that money, resources, and the ones who make the rules cannot reach and see into their hearts and make a difference. Why do we still have people without food, water, and shelter? Why are there so many people who do not have a job and cannot feed their families? Why do we not share our most precious resources such as our land and ourselves to the ones who need it the most? Why do we keep making things worse? How can anyone tell me that we can not make a difference and that by reaching out all our lives would not benefit? All financial markets would be better off; everyone's lives would become healthier, happier, and more meaningful. We all have the power to give, hope, and love.

Hopefully today will be your day to create something more. Hopefully today will be all of our day to change the road we travel. Hopefully we will look at one another and reach out and help our fellow man, woman, child and all that inhabit this glorious place we call Earth. Let us finally find in our hearts the missing key that unlocks a life of dreams that not only will come true but take us from the stale, negative, and sad ways of the fantasy we seem to get caught up in. Your time is today to push past all the negativity you have placed neatly away and break through with fury into the life you so desperately deserve. The time is now, right now, to achieve this. Don't hesitate!

Remember, to me, my life is perfect in a different way than how you view perfection in your life. Take care of yourself first and then spread your wealth with others. Make sure to always go back to yourself as each day will have challenges. Do not wait to work on yourself. Each day you turn away from yourself adds weeks, months, and years to your constant misery. Your inner demons are not a bad thing to have. We all have them as they are the other side of your multi-dimensional self pushing out saying that you have problems that you will have to deal with in one way or another.

Why do we continue to destroy this unlimited beauty that we call Mother Earth? We should be exploring our planet, living passionately, united with all our extended family, and cherishing the spectacular treasures this planet has to offer. Instead, we torture ourselves, families, friends, and others. We spread destruction, hate, and the path of greed and power throughout time. For the generations that say this is not my fault, I have to differ with you. Even if you choose not to believe in reincarnation, today what we do not just affects us now, but in the future generations to come. I believe that we as souls have lived on Earth many times and have been destructive. We have hurt ourselves and our planet time and time again.

We seem to continue to become more destructive on a much larger scale. The Dark Ages were violent for most, but for humans it was a time of uncertainty and most were uneducated. Now the world is easier to be experienced by all. Many people are educated and this should be a time for a certain future of forgiveness, compassion, and love. To me, God's eternal plan was for us to push past this Barbaric way from earlier times. God wants for us to finally learn more loving ways that would bring the human race together as one huge extended family. Why has it taken so long for us to make a difference in our ways? Why are we so trained to the madness and destruction? Why can we not look past our differences and open our hearts and minds to be free from this everlasting nightmare we keep coming back to?

How can we keep telling our children to be kind when we are the ones who keep destroying everything we touch? We want our children to be respectful, to open up and love, to be responsible, to be patient and compassionate. When are we as adults going to show the children the way of peace, love, and forgiveness? How can we expect anyone, especially children to do this if we do not and never try? Adults destroy things and then build them just to repeat the cycle again. We hurt each other senselessly and just fall back into the trap of deceit and anguish. We say we are sorry, then turn around and do the same thing again. When are we going to change? Now? Tomorrow? Next week? Next year? How about this moment, stop the excuses, help yourself, and choose to change, we all deserve the peace and certainty that comes with it.

There is Help Out There

● ● ● ● ●

In our country alone, there are more and more obese people, depressed people, people with anxiety and stress disorders, and people with chronic heart, lung, and liver problems. The world has seen a rise with these and many life threatening conditions. The simple truth is that these and all the addictions that people have can be eliminated through such methods as taking a portion of your day to work on yourself. It would be extremely helpful to understand your ailments and to find a solution to these problems, solve them, and then move on with your life. The problem, most people will say, is that they do not have time. Meditation, yoga, Pilates, Reiki, massage, acupuncture and regression therapy will work wonders for everyone. However, you will need to take the time for the methods listed above to work. These natural life rehabilitating ways will do wonders for you and your human spirit. Reiki is an alternative healing energy that transmits the healer's energy to yours. Healing occurs where your body's energy is not flowing smoothly and in turn symptoms arise. Pilates and yoga controls the muscles and relaxes the mind to control stability from your outer core from within. Meditation alone can take you back to a more loving you, to push away from stress, anxiety, and pain in your life. Most importantly, it will help you take a journey deep within yourself where love, patience, and happiness truly exist. A full body massage once a month or at least a couple of times per year can help you to relax and release your body's toxins that have built up from daily abuse. For more major issues that seem to linger no matter what you have tried, regression therapy is an amazing life changing process that will not mask your problems the way traditional psychology does. It eliminates hardships and pain from this life and others you have had, no matter if you believe in reincarnation or not. This is an amazing experience that I cannot emphasize enough. It is a truly life changing method and it can change every aspect of your being. In cases, this miracle therapy has cured diseases, stopped addictions, extreme anxiety, depression, and many other ailments that people suffer from. This type of therapy actually goes to the root of your problems.

How amazing would our planet be if we would all just help one another and open ourselves up to the reality of the human spirit of love, kindness, and charity? Our health problems are from centuries of abuse, pain, and hate. Just by taking these things out of the equation, humans would finally be able to breathe, love life, and become healthier.

Don't Be Afraid, See the Real You, Clear the Clutter and Hear, See and Feel the Signs

• • • • •

If you would, go to a mirror and take a good look at yourself. While doing so, look at the images created and visualize yourself at your deepest core. The simple fact is that we are souls living in a physical body. Inside, the beauty is contagious; we all look the same from a soul perspective, a loving light that spreads the truth, love, and an eternal bond between all the souls of this reality. If we choose to see from within, we would see that we are all souls moving along together at our own pace but along a path that, in part, God created.

One enormous thing that has helped me on my journey to recover from heartache, sadness, anger, and confusion is noticing signs that are around me. Everyone on this beautiful planet, everyday, every night, even while asleep in our dreams, sees signs in one way or another. When you are stressed, angry, or having negative feelings, you view everything around you like you are looking through a tunnel. You look through one view and do not notice the life that is around you. You basically live your life on auto pilot wondering why years down the road you never noticed all the signs that were shown to you, trying to help you along the way.

This is where guardian angels, spirit guides, and your higher self come in. These spirits are saying, "Hey, big dummy, wake up. I am trying to help you! Stop making the same mistakes. You don't have to punish yourself; you've already done this enough. See what you've missed, start living now and move forward."

Remember that the signs are different for each of us. We are all on our own path that is interconnected with each other. But ultimately it is our choice to think about why we are in the mess in that moment.

When we clear our mind and love from the heart, the signs will come clearer and more often, and will help us along life's uncertain path. We have been given a miracle and that miracle is called life. The signs will become clearer by moving away any and all the distractions and all the negative experiences that weigh us down. It is up to you to want a life that is not stuck in quicksand; a life that has been aggressively stolen from the life you could experience from within. Finally you will learn to see that you are the miracle in your own life. Remember that there is nothing to fear. Yes, it is normal to be scared, but do not give up! Fear is that nagging, pathetic, wimpy voice that tells you that you can't, you shouldn't, and you are not good enough and not strong enough to do something. Tell that voice to take a flying leap. Fear does you, and the world as a whole, no good.

When we ask for signs from up above, from somewhere else, or from within, we often choose not to listen. For most of us, we underestimate the power, strength, and love we have in ourselves to notice these signs. We ask and the answers fall on deaf ears. We seem to never slow down and make it a priority in our busy lives to just simply take the time for ourselves. From time to time everyone has conversations in their mind. These conversations involve what to say, how to react to a situation, how a situation will turn out, and most people have been disappointed by the results. The reason is that we do not clear the clutter from our ego. We keep letting this clutter overpower our lives. This is why we do not take chances on ourselves. We are always waiting for the precise moment and the right time, only for it to pass us by. We need to just believe in ourselves that whatever lays ahead, whatever experiences we go through, and whatever moment we will experience is the right path, the right time, and the right moment. This is what I call being in the moment and this is what I hope we all should strive for. Then we would all be happier with our decisions, the paths we have chosen, and the relationships we are in. This would also help how we view ourselves and the other loving souls that surround us on Earth.

When you finally reach the level within yourself, you finally see the other you. A you that mirrors the same image on the outside, but from the inside you experience the true essence of your existence. An effort of inspiration, honesty, and true inheritance of possibilities beyond your perception of everything you used to believe in. You open yourself to all ideas and opinions and view everything from all viewpoints. The crescendo of power, strength, and love awes you into feeling the all that life's miracle creates for us. This is where you inspire others to reach higher within themselves.

There has been quite a bit of talk lately about 2012. Many people feel that the world will be ending. Look at it this way: if it is going to happen, why not make your life worth living today, because soon it may be over. If it does not happen, why live another moment in pain, confusion, or sadness? No matter what happens, your life is yours to live and to take on the other side. Remember we are here to learn our own lessons. The time for making excuses is over. Stop the madness! It is time to listen to your soul and create the life you can and will have by recreating yourself.

Simplify everything, I mean everything you create in your life. Start believing in yourself. Smile more than you frown, live today because tomorrow may not come. Start giving yourself some credit because each day is difficult, it is supposed to be to learn and to move forward. Remember that we choose everything including our thoughts, opinions, and actions. More importantly, we choose the path we are on, but we can choose another one, and another, and another until we as an individual find the peace, love, and harmony we so desperately need to live an open, caring, and compassionate life. Do not forget to laugh at your mistakes. We all make them; there isn't anyone here on Earth that is perfect. The past is over, the future is not here yet, and you must live in the present. Don't be afraid to take that first step. You are the miracle and this is your time. Stop standing there and make it happen! Laugh often and smile; love much more as this is the key to unlocking every ounce of happiness already instilled in us all! Always be yourself and make your own path. Be the leader of you and open yourself to every experience. Pray, meditate, and believe.

I wish everyone happiness, love, harmony, and a journey that opens every possibility and every door. A journey that tears down all the barriers that are around you; a journey that brings a profound and utmost purity of the dream. The infinite dream that takes you from any heartache you are living now. Today is your day. Move at your own pace, and remember we are all together on this journey, you are never alone. Believe, endure, simplify, and start living!

Afterword

• • • • •

There is a simple way and for you the road will be different than the rest. Each one of you is unique and remarkable in your own exclusive way. Please take the time each day for yourself and enjoy the journey along the way. Today is your day and each step you take will bring you to a clearer more precise outlook within yourself. I wanted to clear up a few things about my writing. Again, my beliefs are my own and my path is my choice. From where I came from to the present is what I definitely call a miracle. The "true self" I talk about is your own unique self, the person who is different from everyone else, but is bonded by everyone else in the world we know and the universe itself. I am lucky and thankful to be writing this and hoping this journey you take will create a loving, more nurturing you along the way. We are connected not just by God's love, but by the brother and sisterhood we share in the miracle of you and me as well as the life we live together as one. Even though there are six billion people on this beautiful planet, everything you do from how small to how big makes a difference to the balance of life around you. Please never give up on you; never give in to the nonsense that keeps you from ever creating the life you always wanted, but you never gave the chance to live. As I stated I'm a spiritualist, this does not mean that I do not believe in religion, I just do not practice it. This is my choice, this may not be yours. I know there's a creator, our father, who is God, who is with us every step of the way. Again, my belief, please have your own; you are unique in your own life, beliefs and ideas. I also know that we have a brother in Jesus who gave up more than we know at this moment and who loves us without boundaries and without hesitation. I also know in my heart there are an infinite number of spirits that help guide us along our own loving path. Your beliefs are your very own; this is why they are so blessed in their own meaning.

Poetry, Quotes & Books

● ● ● ● ●

Here are the poems, quotes and books I promised you…

"Love is the affinity which links and draws together the elements of the world."

"A dream will always triumph over reality, once it is given a chance."

"Believe the best in yourself."

"The more you praise and celebrate your life, the more there is in life to celebrate."

"Happiness is the experience of living every minute with love, grace and gratitude."

"Think lovingly, speak lovingly, act lovingly."

"Give of yourself to someone who needs you."

"Bring your life to life; stop planning, start doing."

"Don't judge others or yourself."

"Kick a bad habit for today."

"Make plans, but allow for changes."

"Think without limits."

"In life's winter, find your invincible summer." From Linda in New York

"Love yourself, dare to dream, live on purpose." From Dana in Highland, IN

"Keep moving forward; don't look back." From Sally in Griffith, IN

"When you can't control the wind, adjust your sails!" From Brenda in Schofield, WI

"Celebrate the small victories in your life." From Debbie in Fairfield, OH

"It's OK to not do it all." From Dawn in Wildwood, MO

"Love the person in the mirror before anyone else." From Joan in Pawtucket, RI

"Life does have 'do-over's.'" From Sharon in St. Joseph, MO

"Do not regret not loving in the past, the past is over. Begin right now; it's never too late to express your love and compassion." Brian L. Weiss, M.D.

"Forgive the past. It is over. Learn from it and let go. Do not cling to a negative image of a person in the past. See that person now. Your relationship is always alive and changing." Brain L. Weiss, M.D.

"All is love. With love comes understanding, with understanding comes patience. And the time stops…and everything is now." Brian L. Weiss, M.D.

"Love is the ultimate answer. Love is not an abstraction but an actual energy…which you can "create" and maintain in your being. Love dissolves fear. You cannot be afraid when you are feeling love. Since everything is energy, and love encompasses all energies…all is love." Brain L. Weiss, M.D.

"We ask for rewards and justifications for our behaviors… when there are no rewards, the reward is in doing, but doing without expecting anything…doing unselfishly." Brian L. Weiss, M.D.

"Never is hate diminished by hatred. It is only diminished by love." Bruce Lee

"When you look into the eyes of another, any other, and you see your own soul looking back at you, then you will know you have a reached another level of consciousness." Brian L. Weiss, M.D.

"Patience and timing…everything comes when it must come. A life cannot be rushed, cannot be worked on a schedule as so many of us want it to be. We must accept what comes to us at a given time, and not ask for more. We pass through different phases. But time is not as we see time, but rather in lessons that are learned." Brian L. Weiss, M.D.

"Too often we underestimate the power of a touch, a smile, a kind word, a listening ear, an honest compliment, or the smallest act of kindness, all of which have the potential to make someone happier or to turn a life around." Unknown

"A human being is part of the whole we call the universe, a part limited in time and space. He or she experiences there selves, there thoughts and feelings as something separated from the rest…a kind of optical illusion of his or her consciousness. This illusion is a prison for us, restricting us to our personal desires and to affection for only the few people nearest us. Our task must be to free our circle of compassion, to embrace all living beings and all of nature." Albert Einstein

"I have learned how important it is to tell the people when you love them, because tomorrow is just a concept in our minds." Ryan J. Robinson… Spoken by him the night before he passed on.

Follow the Wind
Follow the Wind to other sides that call for you.
Can you capture the life that has yet to be lived?
That stained soul can be cleaned with Time and Faith.

Ryan J. Robinson

Resources

• • • • •

Here are some books that helped me; maybe they will help you.

Mitch Albom
    For one more day
    Have a Little Faith
    Tuesdays with Morrie
    The Five People you Meet in Heaven

April Crawford
    Inner Whispers: Messages from a Spirit Guide

Brian L. Weiss, M.D.
    Through Time into Healing
    Only Love is Real
    Messages from the Masters
    Same Soul, Many Bodies

WM. Paul Young
    The Shack

About the Author

• • • • •

A little about me, I grew up in the Detroit area, along with my parents, younger sister, older brother and older sister. We had our difficult moments and good times as well. I was closest to my older sister growing up, though I hung out with my older brother at times especially during our Boy Scout trips. I became closer to my younger sister as an adult. My mother worked as a hairstylist and stayed home taking care of her family. My father worked most of the time; his job was and still is a mechanical engineer. Back then, times were tough as they are now, but looking back, I strongly believe everything happened the way it was suppose to for each of us to learn our own ways and to grow into the individuals we are now. It is never good to be hurt or to experience sadness, pain, or any negative emotion, but that is what makes us stronger as souls. I grew up with many friends, a lot of them were very close to me and some still are. I was a goofy kid, very shy at first, but if you got to know me, my energetic side would prevail. I was hurt quite a bit going through life and as time went on, I let it turn me into a more depressed, sad, and confused younger adult. I turned to alcohol at a young age and this of course did not help matters. It eventually brought out my darker side and put me into a tail spin of negative, hurtful acts that turned my world from just getting by into a severe depressed state that spiraled out of control for the better part of twenty years. At times I was out of control and I hurt a lot of loving people along the way. Thankfully, times have changed and I had the strength to overcome these dark emotions that I let over take me. I had symptoms such as anxiety attacks that would paralyze me and night terrors that pushed me to my limit. It was impossible to have a good night's rest back then. I would also go into rages that would devastate anyone who was near me. These rages would come and go, but they got worse as I entered my thirties. These rages were mostly vocal, but they were devastating just the same. As I have stated, if you do not take the time to figure yourself out now, whatever is locked away in your brain will show its ugly self whether you like it or not. The longer you wait, the stronger these emotions will grow. The beginning of my healing journey started with me helping children with hard lives themselves. Working with these souls opened my eyes, heart and soul to what I have come to know now is a life worth living. I am currently an educator who works with special needs children in Central New York. I am blessed every day even when I lose sight of the path I am on. I have beautiful, caring and compassionate souls in my life, which I thank the heavens above to have as friends, companions and as soul mates. I wanted to personally thank the souls that never gave up on me and helped me through my pain, struggles and sadness. With time, everything heals; you just have to take that first step.